The Weeping Rose

(To Dream)

Author: Janet L. Foster
Photographer: Barbara A. Foley

The Weeping Rose (To Dream)

Author copyrighted © 2008 Janet L. Foster
Photography copyrighted © 2008 Barbara A. Foley

All rights reserved by the author and photographer. No copy's or use of any material in this book without the permission from the author or photographer.

Printed by Lulu Enterprises, Inc.

All Rights Reserved

For more information:
http://www.lulu.com

Janet L. Foster, Huntingdon, PA
Barbara A. Foley, Bellefonte, PA

Online at http://lv2scpbk.blogspot.com

ISBN 978-0-6152-1440-5

Acknowledgments

I want to thank my husband, Dennis Foster for encouraging me to finish my book. Also, I would like to thank my children, Holly and Roger, for proof reading my poems and giving me constructive criticism. Finally, I would like to thank my sister, Barbara Foley for giving me that extra push and doing the photos for this book. The photos will give the extra edge to understanding each and everyone of my poems. Thanks to everyone that believed in me.

Janet L. Foster

I want to thank my husband, John, whom never minds all my endless photo taking, my two boys, Luke and Mitch, and especially my grandson, Landon, who always let's me know when there is a good photo opportunity. I would also like to thank my sister, Janet Foster for giving me the opportunity to include my photos in her book. Finally, I would like to thank everyone who has visited my blog and gave me feedback on my photos.

Barbara A. Foley

Contents

Memories of Once Loved	3
The Rock	5
The Veil Upon My Face	7
In My Dream World	9
Of Lonely Times	11
Just For You	13
A Promise of Love	15
Need For a Fantasy	17
At Heaven's Gate	19
I'll Be Your Guardian Angel	21
On a Sparrow's Wing	23
Broken Hearts	25
Love's Chance	27
Within My Diary	29
Breath of Sunshine	31
Quest of True Love	33
This Man of Mine	35
The Wolf	37
Somewhere Above	39
Broken Love / Shattered Dreams	41
Little Boy Thoughts	43
Wind n the Leaves	45
Like a Butterfly	47
Pebble in the Sand	49

Contents

Blue Feathers & Painted Wolf	51
Empty Pasture	53
Tears of a Rose!	55
The Weeping Rose (Believe)	57
My Spotted Dream Catcher (The True Story)	59
Fear	61
Truth Untold	63

Special Section of Seasons

Feelings of Love- (A Special Valentine)	67
A Mother's Day Poem	69
Stages of a Child	71
December	73

Memories of Once Loved

One night of pleasure, passion, and
Sincere aggression,
A love never forgotten
A face of truth, and
Wanting of belonging
To now, find out,
It's just a fantasy
Not a legacy
To be mine, No!
To just have it for so long!
Yet still, be in love…
Now it's gone,

Gone…

The Rock

In a world of hardened things
To be tough is a manly admission
For me, I try to build my wall
But at times it's hard to be strong
When there's always someone there
To melt the stones
So I now have a better way
I built my wall, it's not me at all
I have my rock, Thanks to you!
I'm a monument now
And you can not and will not
Bring me down!!

The Veil Upon My Face

As I lay upon the dampened ground
By waters edge, and stars abound
As foggy haze lifts skyward
And morning dew drips from the leaves
The veil I wear upon my face
Is like the foggy mist of summers, grew
For as hardened as things seem to be
I still believe is lover's fate
To see your face, is this the path
I will remain!
To live this life of willing vain
Not be that Juliet, like so many times
How can these things be left untold
I wait and wait, his heart so cold
To see the Lord, to ask in vain
For him to see the truth unfold
The love I have for him to hold!

In My Dream World

Kings and Queens
Princesses & Princes
Where's my knight in shining
There's just a minute of timing
I've lived a life of waiting, Hoping
For that one special love
Will he come?
No! I think not
I close my eyes
And dream of these things
And wake up to a scary
Reality!

Of Lonely Times

What do you do?
What do you say?
Like a flower that wilts
On a hot summer day
So does a love gone astray
When there's no nourishment
To rekindle the flame
It feels like being homesick
So far…far…Away!
To have faith is to love him
I'm no longer sure!
So full of loneliness, don't know
What to do!

Just For You!

Just for you, I write this poem
The meanings are from my heart and soul!
Let me be the air you breathe,
The warmth you feel upon your face
Are the rays of light you give to me
From each morning's kiss!
The sparks it makes are like fireworks
Within my heart
And, if yours is broke
Let me be,
Cupids arrow to mend the break,
For you, just for you,
I'll do all these things,
For if I have your heart,
Mine will be big enough, to carry us through.
I Love You…!

A Promise of Love

I love you with all my heart
But, you show nothing but hardness.
To feel your chest against mine,
Fills me with warmth and sadness
Knowing your heart isn't mine.
I have so much love built up inside,
To let it out,
To share with you beside me
You are so hardened of things behind us,
Toughened and blinded by all that pain!
I am on a mission for your submission,
I've been so eager to have, your love again
For ecstasy to abound with us again!
As it shall, I do proclaim!
I will lavish and joyfully,
Love you till there's no more pain!
As this I know, you are all that I know,
We'll be once again and the birds will sing,
It'll feel like spring, Once again!

Need For A Fantasy

The tightness of my chest
And, the voices in my head
The unanswered question of my wish
Hollow feelings in the pit of my stomach
Turns, Turns, All because of you
Answers I seek, Answers to see
The look in your eyes,
So distant and deep
The touch of your hand
Arms wrapped around me,
Not like so many times before
A need for a fantasy,
To be your torch of flames beyond
For you to hold and adore
So we can be one,
And, never let go
Yes, I am in love!
Yet, am so lonely and blue
Where is the sparkle, far into your heart,
To let it out, to shine for me
Could be the greatest fantasy
You could have for me!
Oh! Yes, I'm in love with you!
Could you be in love with me too!
Oh! This is the fantasy I need to hold on to!

At Heavens Gate

For him I'll wait, Tis my mistake
How can I make the things go away?
Those haunting sounds so deep in my head
Of all the mistakes and wrongs I've done
I stand at the gate, so blue am I
And can't believe, my heads so high
I turned around and still no you
To let me down when you even knew
The only one that didn't let me down
Has always been there, even in the clouds
His big brown eyes, weeping like blue
I wouldn't blame him if he turned from me
Through thick and thin I know this true
He'll still be there
To see me through!!

I'll Be Your Guardian Angel

You say your looking for your guardian angel
And, you believe there's one for everyone
But, then you're sure of angels at all!
Look to me and you will see,
Let me be the guardian angel you seek!
I know things are tough, and we've been through a lot,
If only you could see, through my eyes what I see!
I would do all that I can, even carry you cross land,
And, if only I had wings, we could fly over the sea
On wings of snow white, and hearts of fire,
No more worries or heartache for you at all!
I'd weather the storm and carry the load,
If only you could see through my eyes, what I see!
Please…give me a sign of your love for me!
And, let me be your guardian angel you seek!
Promises made are promises kept,
Let this be, our dedication of our love!
Then together forever, we'll make stars up above,
Then again you'll believe in us, and our love once again!
So, shed no more tears,
And, let go of your fears,
Now open your heart,
Let your love shine through, like you've always wanted to do!
Cause, your guardian angel is already here!
…Just to love you!

On a Sparrows Wing

My heart is heavy
Laded with sadness
I look to the sky for answers unseen
Like the sparrows fly, up on their wings
To soar high in the sky
Be free and serene
And, when the rain falls
It will be me you see,
For all my fears, I've had
Will fall down from the clouds
Accumulating…Accumulating…
From years gone by
What you see, like a river flows
Be filled with tears, of all my woes!

Broken Hearts

Of the nights that are so still
You hear the weeps of a whippoorwill
She isn't asleep, she has no will
For her heart still bleeds, it's broken still.
Her love so deep, the feelings of pain,
I know how she feels!
The pain and anguish
I have instilled, in my true loves heart,
His unanswered questions of truth and love,
To be together is all I want
Of compassion and understanding needed for each other,
I will be sorry forever more
I cannot change it, and if I could
I'd be in his debt, for his love,
From his heart of steel,
To have one wish, this wish,
For his broken heart to heal!

Love's Chance

The love we can share
Isn't always fair
But, as some things fall
They can also rise
Give it a chance
And, You will find
As the sunset falls across the sky
And, the sunrise rises over the sea
You can count on my love
It will always rise!
We can share the rainbow,
Across the sky!
The soothing sound of the water
Bouncing against the waters edge
We'll never give up,
We'll never be bored!
There's always something new and challenging too!
Like a new born baby
Being born in the spring,
So can our love grow,
We can always be free
We'll shine only together
Like the stars in the midnight sky!
We'll lie under the moon
Always, to have a natural high
We'll only need us, under the big blue sky!

Within My Diary

Do you really want to know?!
Do you really want to learn,
The real pain that's within!
Have you ever really walked in the rain,
The rain of tears that never stop!
Then, step within my diary,
We'll talk!
We'll walk!
We'll even share the pain!
I've known the hurt,
The everyday pain,
The loss of a loved one,
That's gone away,
Gone!
But not forgotten, page after page!
And, then there's love!
Only something to relish and think of…
Hope for!
Wish for!
And, maybe, just maybe, someday have!
Within my diary…
Will you help me through?!

Breath of Sunshine

To the world at hand
That I will never lie
The breath I take
Should fill me like sunshine,
The man I love,
He should be my friend
For maybe then, I would get,
More out of him!
His scent fills me with warm love
Oh! I miss him so much!
Miss him, His touch,
The laughter we shared
Oh! It's getting tough!
If you should find him,
Send him back to me
I miss that breath of sunshine,
He used to give to me!
For I truly do love him,
Like he used to love me!

**Quest of True Love
"Search for His Heart"**

When the sun shines, peaceful and serene
When the water flows, just to be seen
Some of these things, we never ask why
When we ask of love, we look to the sky!
Into the deep dark blue, I ask…Why?
My one true love, within himself
Never lets his love, down from the shelf
How did we come to this, this time of doubt?
The tears that fall, come from a cloud
To fog our minds, in this time of doubt
To sit in a field, I shout to let it out!
Look at the sky, I ask why?
Oh!…Why can't we have wings and fly!
Our hearts could sing,
If you could only believe,
Why can't you, just let your love out!
Let it fly! Like the birds in the sky,
Let it be known!
Like the sun glows!
To search the world over,
Is not what I need
For you to show me,
It's me that you need!
Till then, It's my quest to search for his heart!!

This Man of Mine

I feel the sadness,
And, the emptiness
The special love we once shared,
Has gone away, and lays dormant somewhere
His shattered heart,
I broke without thought!
Oh! How I wish I could fix things like this!
My love for him, just grows and grows
The sorrow I feel,
Like cancer grows
My heart is heavy,
Both day and night,
Just thinking of this man,
This man of mine!
How can this last?
This broken heart
I look to the heavens,
The questions I ask,
Will his heart ever mend?
And, will he love me again!

The Wolf
(His Thoughts, His Pride)

Run with the wolf
His thoughts, his pride
Look deep, so deep into his sad gloomy eyes!
You will only then see his deep-set pride
A pride so strong, searching…
With courage, he roams to hide,
Hide? He too feels love, down inside!
I feel, I too need his thoughts and pride
To have such courage, hidden love inside
So, then we could soar, together forever
Our love and pride as our guide
Feelings…The Wolf?!
His thoughts and his pride
Love…?!
Thought as of nothing, Just
The still of the night!
If I could run with the wolf,
Love hidden deep inside!
Run with the wolf!!
Don't let our love die!
Hidden…Hidden
Deep inside!
Could this be a question,
That the wolf might ask?
To look in his face,
He has lots to ask!
But, still again…thoughts and pride
Get in the way…Again!
See through his eyes…
With shoulders high!

Somewhere Above
(I Ask Why?)

Why! Can't things be the way
They used to be,
We used to walk in the woods
You and me!
Why! Can't I feel love the way,
You used to make me feel,
By the things you used to say!
I know there's an answer to this
Not just an imagination, uninterrupted
Yearning of mine!
I can show you how I feel
Climb that next hill,
And fly so high in the sky!
Oh, If only I could take your hand,
We could soar, together across the land,
Never worry what others think,
And, in a wink,
Like a magical being,
Open our eyes, need not ask why,
Like magic, somewhere above,
Yes! We'll feel the same!
Love, again will reign!

Broken Love/Shattered Dreams

His hair of chocolate brown
Streaks of silver gray abounds
The sadness whispers through, his eyes of brown
Shattered dreams and emptiness
Feelings of love once known,
To this shell of a man,
Taken away, his broken love
Of no less,
The woman he worshiped for so many years!
She knew him well,
His dreams and fears
She took his hand, He was her man.
He loved her so,
Oh! Where did it go?
Mistakes were made,
Both were wrong
Can this be mended,
Will it take too much time!
The hearts unwind,
Can he again be mine?
This broken man
This saddened woman,
Both love each other, still,
Too proud to let their feelings show
Questions asked,
Answers unfound!
If they could look to each other
The answers are there
Cling to each other, Once again for what they need
This broken man, and saddened woman,
Their dreams of love to share
Their ups and downs, can come to pass
Look to the stars,
For their love to last!
They are one, though they don't know it yet,
For I am that saddened woman,
I'll always regret!

Little Boy Thoughts

We go for a walk,
Then what do I see!
A little boy walking,
His head down
Just back a few feet,
Pappy, in front, Looking at trees.
The little boy, his hat down, then with a sideways smile
Kicks a stone,
Looks like skipping across the water
But, it's a path you see!
Next thing I see,
Looking up with that crooked smile
Wouldn't you like to know?
What he's really thinking?
I would!
It's a train he see's!
Glossy eyes, he holds his mouth
Pap, Do you see what I see?
He stands and looks,
As it passes by,
Did he ever choose?
The path he chose?
The path for him,
In his eyes
The sparkle of life
We rarely see!

Wind in The Leaves

Wind in the leaves,
Just the sound of the breeze!
Someone is knocking, it sounds like trees
Come with me, and you will see!
It's someone else, looks like me!
If I could only see, and smell the fresh green trees!
I would only be, a root!
A small fresh seedling you see!
That, is what I want
To be!

Like a Butterfly

I wish you would capture me
Like a butterfly!
Would admire me if I were beautiful,
Like a butterfly with golden wings!
Treat me as I were delicate,
Make me feel like it was spring!
And everyday whisper and caress me
Then I could sing!
But, I know this is only a dream,
I can only daydream of all these things!
And, if you really knew how I feel!
You would try and wish all your will,
Make all these dreams, so very real!
And, like a butterfly with injured wings,
So, very lost and alone through spring!
Once again with his thoughts of love,
Find that one and only lost true love!
Like a butterfly, this once in a lifetime thing!
Like a butterfly,
Needing true love!

Pebble in The Sand

In his arms only,
And me alone!
Why am I…All alone!
In this world,
I feel like a stone!
A pebble in the sand…
Find me!
It's so hard to see,
When everything is the same,
In all this pain!
Love me!
Can't you see?
Tell me!
It's only me you need!
Like a stone, I'll always be…
The only pebble you may see,
All alone, down by the sea!

Blue Feathers & Painted Wolf

She sits by the lake
So forlorn and exhausted
Her blue feathers blowing in the breeze
Like the silence in her gaze
Waiting while her tears fill the lake...
Waiting...Waiting...
For her true love to come back to her...
Painted wolf...her one true love,
Her tears still come,
While still filling the lake
As she gazes and watches for painted wolf
So thin and frail as the night moves on,
The only one to hear her whispers is the wind,
Rustling through the feathers in her hair...
As dawn moves in
A sparkle begins! ...
As she holds the blue feathers in her hand,
She thinks back of the bond,
Between painted wolf and her,
And when it all began!

Empty Pasture

Do you believe in fate?
If only I closed the gate!
I looked up the hill,
Became ill, …
Their not there, I can only stare…
I miss them like they miss me!,
Home is where the heart is,
And, their hearts are with me, here
Where they call, home!
Their tails flowing, their hooves pounding,
They whinny…they know they are home!
To love, they know, to cry, we know!
An empty pasture, an empty home
Is the same and something we've all known
In our hearts, come home!
We ask, they ask?
Please, Please come home!
Once again, we can roam…!
The horses we are, sturdy and strong
Our heart's desire is to be loved,
At home!

Tears of a Rose!

Like a rosebud waking to the morning dew,
Forming a tear for me and you,
An awakening, surprisingly, blossoming to,
Something more beautiful than the moon at night!...
Then, again, sadness overcomes the day when reality sets in,
and saves the day?
But, it's only a gaze, a dream, like a stream
It flows in the breeze, ...
Like leaves on trees,
Can't you see it's my tears you see! ...
Like the tears of a rose!
For you and me
Cause we try to please,
And never leave!
Like the tears of a rose
Then blossoms for all to see,
Then wilts of sadness
Like the world is to me,
For that tear on that rose,
Belongs to me!

The Weeping Rose
(Believe)

Like butterfly wings, each petal in shape
Beauty abounds, with each breath you take
Rays from the sun, peeking through the clouds,
Just standing there, brings your eyes down.
Look a little closer, a pixie near me!
In the morning dew, so hard to see,
Then in the mist, ...
Bending down on just one knee
Seeing droplets of dew on the petals of the rose
Looks like tear drops to me!
As I watched, the tear drops fall,
A whisper of hope after all!
To see a weeping rose all alone,
In an empty pasture where they used to roam
But, then a little pixie voice cries out,
But, it is winter not spring! ...
To see the weeping rose,
The rose, which you seek,
Gives you the hope,
To believe!

My Spotted Dream Catcher
(The True Story)

The first time I saw him
There he was, standing at the far end of the pasture…
…all alone
The first time I rode him, and then I knew
All this guy wanted was a chance
You could tell by his eyes in a glance
The love he longed for, just give him a chance!
All those glorious spots and personality
The love he shows!
If he could only talk, "Take me home!"
Shy and demure he looked, but feared
It was only a dream, could anyone? …
Love him, No…Only me!
But listen to him, I did!
Now he's loved and has a home,
With me!
My spotted dream catcher
So special to me!

Fear

Eyes of snake eyed brown
Locked in as if there was no sound!
Hear the tick of heart,
No, the asking abounds…
Hear the question? …
Will you? …Could you? …
Be the mission to astound!
Please me?
Don't know...Looks like you could
If I only knew!
Please you, yes I would,
If I could,
Fear is within
If you only knew!
Save me!
I would…you! …
My brown eyes see only you,
Merlin!

Truth Untold

Love could only be, a truth untold!
If only you knew,
Love is held by you alone,
No! …By two…young and old
But…the tell doesn't stop at human alone
Listen, stop and embrace
What you hold,
Trust and love then unfolds
Move on and still,
Ones embrace unfolds
Fear!
Listening!
When…you listen
Listen…you think
Maybe,
Then, you just heard!

Special Section Of Seasons

Feelings of Love-A Special Valentine

To my love, true love
To love so much
To feel your touch,
You make me feel, like summers breeze
We could fly high in the sky
On a sparrows wing,
For without you near me,
I could never be
You are what I want,
And, always will need!
I love you so much
Please…Always love me!
You'll never know,
I could never say
The feelings inside
I feel each day,
My love is so deep
I can no longer sleep or eat
I could melt the snow
On a cold winters day,
As long as you are near me
And promise, never to leave
I will always be,
In love with you,
You mean that much to me!
And you'll always be, A Valentine to Me!!

A Mother's Day Poem

I honor my mother, who's sometimes tough
The need for her love, at times was rough!
She always listened when I needed to talk,
I'll even remember those little walks!
Her soft spoken voice, full of assurance
Her audacity of life is her encouragement!

The love of the outdoors,
Can be seen in her hands,
When she's happiest of all, out working the land!

Her hands are tough, her heart is warm
To relax is something she has not known,
Like the birds that fly and squirrels roam,
The rest for her is to work at home!

For all these reasons, not many has known,
She is my mother, and I sincerely love her!
With a wish for her to be happy,
On Mother's Day!

Stages of a Child

A baby to hold,
A child of praise,
The joy to hold at any age
Somebody's child,
At any stage!
May good times be,
May bad times…SEIZE!
My child to me,
Is now a mother to be,
Her joys to hold,
Always, A child to me!
Stages of a child
Blessed are we!

December

The snow
The cheer
All turned gloomy in one year!
What happened to the good one,
We used to know?
Seasons do change,
As so do we!
Last minute shoppers, as are we,
Love shines a light,
A glimmer, just a speck!
A few days before Christmas
It happens one night
It has nothing to do with Christmas,
Or does it?
God …Sends the glimmer of hope
For our love to grow!

www.ingramcontent.com/pod-product-compliance
Lightning Source LLC
Chambersburg PA
CBHW021023090426
42738CB00007B/876